I0421906

THE BUSHCRAFT HANDBOOKS

TRAVEL & GEAR

Illustrations by the Author

Richard H. Graves

The Bushcraft Handbooks
Travel & Gear

This Edition Copyright © 2013 by Palmer River Publishing

Cover, Graphics and Layout by: Palmer River Publishing

ISBN-13: 978-1484822531
ISBN-10: 1484822536

About The Author

The author of "The Bushcraft Handbooks", Richard Graves, is a member of the Irish literary family of that name.

A veteran of the Great War campaigns in the Dardenelles and the Western Front, the author became passionate about the bush at an early age. As an enthusiastic bushwalker, skier and pioneer of white-water canoeing, he foresaw how a knowledge of bushcraft could save lives in the Second World War. To achieve this end, he initiated and led the Australian Jungle Rescue Detachment, assigned to the Far East American Air Force. This detachment of 60 specially selected A.I.F. soldiers successfully effected more than 300 rescue missions, most of which were in enemy-held territory in New Guinea, without failure of a mission or loss of a man.

An essential preliminary for rescue was survival, and it was for this purpose that the notes for these books were written. These notes were later revised and prepared for a School in Bushcraft which has been operating for several years and continues to provide valuable instruction to Servicemen embarking overseas on active service in Korea and Malaya.

Bushcraft

As far as is known, "The Bushcraft Handbooks" are unique. There is nothing quite like them, nor is any collection of published bushcraft knowledge as comprehensive.

The term "Bushcraft" is used because "woodcraft" commonly means either knowledge of local fauna and flora or else is associated with the blood-sports of hunting and shooting. "The Bushcraft Handbooks" include a volume on traps and snares, but these are purposely-designed to be completely ineffective for native animals which are insect enters or grazers. These traps have been included because they would only be effective in catching predatory animals such as cats and dogs which have taken to the bush, and other "pest" creatures such as feral swine or goat.

"Bushcraft" describes the activity of how to make use of natural materials found locally in any area. It includes many of the skills used by primitive man, and to these are added "white man" skills necessary for survival, such as time and direction, and the provision of modern "white man" comforts as illustrated in the volume on bush campcraft.

The practice of bushcraft develops in an individual a remarkable ability to adapt quickly to a changing environment. Because this is so, the activity is a valuable counter to the over-specialisation so prevalent in today's society, and is particularly significant in youth training and character-moulding work.

INTRODUCTION to the BUSHCRAFT HANDBOOKS

THE PRACTICE OF BUSHCRAFT shows many unexpected results. The five senses are sharpened, and consequently the joy of being alive is greater.

The individual's ability to adapt and improvise is developed to a remarkable degree. This in turn leads to increased self-confidence.

Self-confidence, and the ability to adapt to a changing environment and to overcome difficulties, is followed by a rapid improvement in the individual's daily work. This in turn leads to advancement and promotion.

Bushcraft, by developing adaptability, provides a broadening influence, a necessary counter to offset the narrowing influence of modern specialisation.

For this work of bushcraft all that is needed is a sharp cutting implement: knife, axe or machete. The last is the most useful. For the work, dead materials are most suitable. The practice of bushcraft conserves, and does not destroy, wild life.

R.H.G.
April, 1952

CONTENTS

TRAVEL & GEAR

It may be necessary to travel through unknown country, and this, without map, compass or any equipment. Under some conditions the traveller may have been totally unprepared and on his ability to travel and arrive may depend his ultimate survival.

In this book a little known or used ability of the eyes to stereoscope aerial or other pairs of photographs, and view the subject in true three dimensions, unaided by any optical equipment, has been included. Under some conditions this knowledge may be useful.

Apart from this, the exercise itself is a valuable and exiting experience in the use of the eyes.

There are many suggestions in this book that will provide real opportunities for adventure, which could be simply doing ordinary things differently.

Travel and gear is of necessity directly associated with the Handbook titled "Time and Direction".

Maps

Before you set out on any journey through the bush you must have a map of the area or else you must make one as you go along.

A map is a plan of a section of country. Being a plan it is drawn to a scale or proportion, and thus is nearly always shown prominently, generally at the foot of the map. As a plan it should also show either TRUE North, MAGNETIC North, or both, which by convention is generally at the top of the map. Unfortunately this useful convention is not always followed, and therefore you must check your map if the North is not shown. If it is not marked you must add this essential information. Show TRUE North as a strong line and MAGNETIC as a dotted line and mark each, so that anyone else using your map will know the difference.

Being a plan of a section of the country, your map will show ground features such as rivers and mountain ranges in relation to one another, and it may show man-made features such as buildings, roads and railways.

Aerial Photos

An alternative to a map is an aerial photograph of the country, or better still, aerial pairs of photographs. To read either an aerial photograph or aerial pairs you must learn to hold them correctly.

With aerial photographs but not necessarily with aerial pairs, the shadows must fall towards you as you look at the photograph.

If you hold an aerial photograph upside down, that is with the shadows falling away from you, you will almost certainly read hills as valley, and vice versa.

Aerial pairs if looked at stereoscopically must be looked at in a special manner, but if a single one of an aerial pair is being studied, it must be viewed with the shadows falling towards you. This is important.

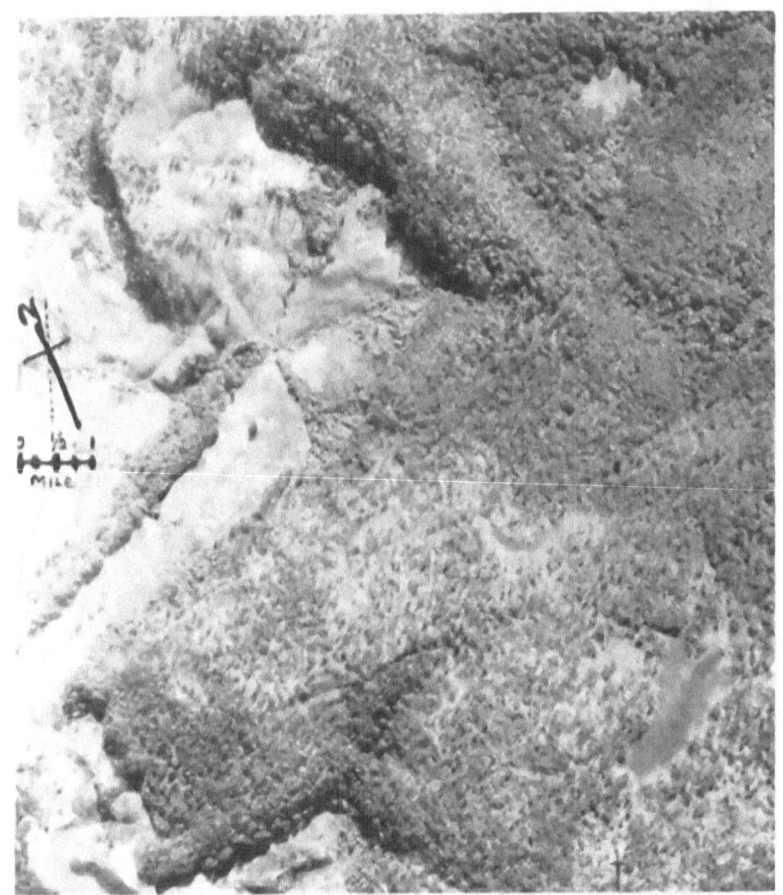

- Photo U.S.A.A.F.

In this aerial the shadows fall towards you, and you can "see" the mountain ranges. Turn it upside down, now the hills become valleys, and the valleys hills.

An aerial photo can give more information than is commonly given on a map, but you must be specially skilled in reading" the photograph, and it takes a real expert to look at a photo and say, "That is ploughed land, and that is forest land, while that is grass country."

The texture of the earth's surface photographed tells the story to the eye of the expert.

3

Stereoscopic Viewing of Aerial Photos

This is true too of aerial pairs. These are photos taken hundreds of feet apart while the plane is flying several thousand feet above the ground. When looked at stereoscopically the mountains and the valleys show form in full three dimension. You can stereoscope these pairs with your eyes alone, unaided by any mechanical means, provided you have two points of vision, that is provided that there is equal or nearly equal vision in both your eyes. The stereoscopic effect is obtained by making each eye see a different image.

The easiest way for you to do this at first is to roll two pieces of paper into tubes about ten inches long and one inch diameter. The exact size is not critical.

Put one tube to your left eye, and place it a few inches over the left eye picture (see last paras, of this section to know how to recognise left eye picture and right eye picture). Now place the other tube to your right eye, with the other end of the tube a few inches above the right eye picture. The two pictures must be side by side, and identical spots on each picture must not be more than three inches apart.

Each eye will see a different image, and with a slight exercise that feels rather like "crossing your eyes" you will see the two pictures merge together, and by concentrating on the single image when they come together you will suddenly see it become fully stereoscopic. (Try and bring the two black dots on each picture together.)

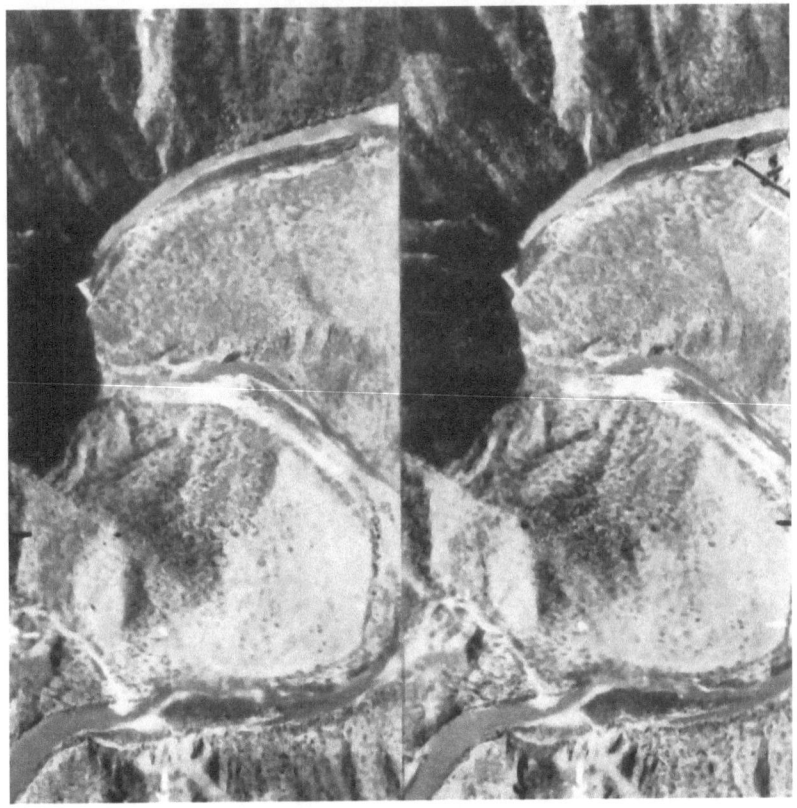

- Photo U.S.A.A.F

Correctly paired.

    This is an eye exercise which at first will make your eyes rather tired, but keep it up. The exercise is good for your eyes, and soon you will be able to look at a pair without tubes and fuse the two images instantly. Try it with tubes on these two pictures. The photo is of a mountain gorge in Dutch New Guinea.

    When you have trained your eyes to see each image through the paper tubes you can take the tubes away, and hold the stereoscoped image in your vision.

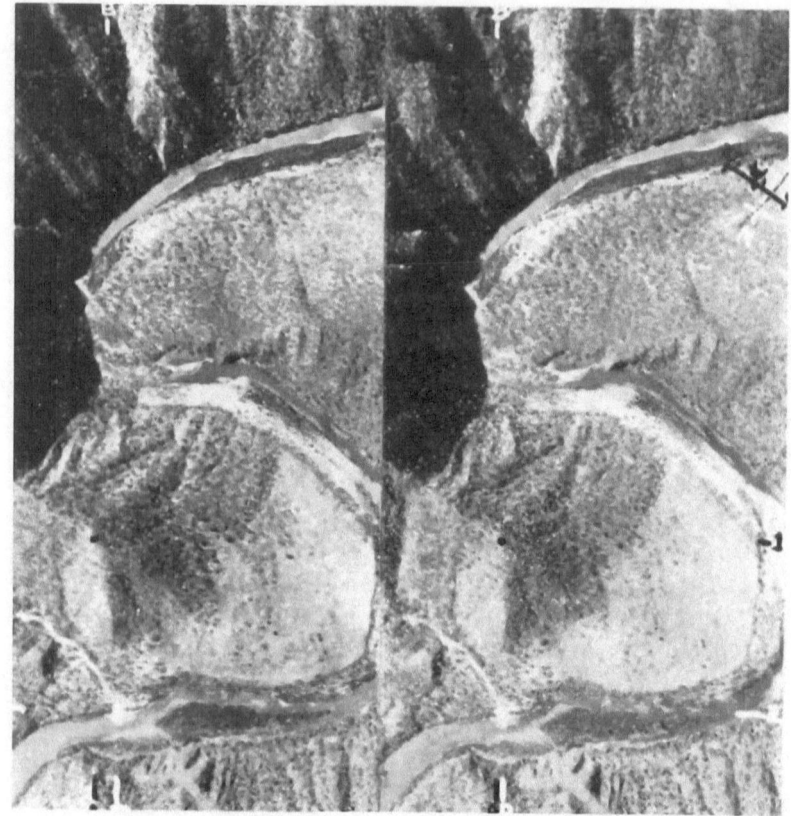

- Photo U.S.A.A.F.

Incorrectly paired.

In stereoscopic use of aerial pairs you must know how to recognise right eye from left eye pictures. If by chance you reverse the images the mountain crests will be deep craters, and the valleys will be ranges. Here is the same stereoscopic pair reversed, viewed stereoscopically you will see this happen.

Note too that in reading stereoscopic pairs it is not necessary for the shadow to fall towards you.

Recognition of Right and Left Stereoscopic Pictures

To discover which is the left eye image select two identifiable points similar in each photo of the pair. One is the black spot on the line YY crossline 1 on the end of the mountain range, and the other is the white spot to the right where the little river joins the main stream on the line XX crossline 2.

One of these points must be on what would be one of the points of highest elevation of the land, and the other on one of the lowest elevations. The two points must be as close to a vertical line as practical. The parallax will show you which is the right and left eye image. In the left image Y and X are closer than in the right image.

Explanation: The parallax is the angle between the point nearest to and the point farthest from the camera. Compare this with same photos reversed. Notice the space between A and B in both photos. In the left image A and B are further apart than in the right image.

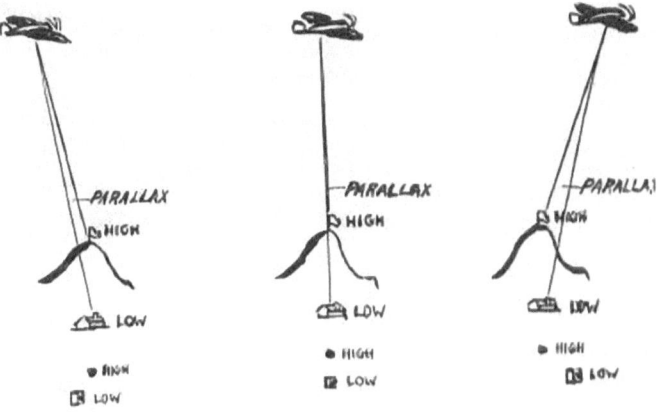

The two pictures must be equal in density of print, and must be placed side by side to be viewed. The maximum distance between two points for comfortable stereoscopic viewing with unaided eyes should not be more than three inches; by straining you may be able to fuse separations four inches apart.

- Photo Reg Perier

NOTE: You can make three dimensional pictures with an ordinary single lens camera by taking two pictures from different positions with exactly the same exposure and aperture. The distance between the two positions is governed by the distance of the nearest object in the foreground from the camera. For every thirty feet the nearest part of the foreground is distant there should be not less than nine inches, and not more than one foot separation in position.

Route From Aerial Photo

When deciding a route from an aerial photo, or from an aerial stereoscopic pair which you have stereoscoped it is essential that you mark the TRUE North on the photo and also determine a scale. The scale will probably be approximate, but it should be sufficiently close to give you not more than half a mile error per five miles of travel.

It is also advisable to prepare a route or sketch map

based on your study of the aerial photo or pair. If you do this you will work to your sketch map, and only refer to your aerial when some point of doubt arises.

Logging Your Route, and Making a Chart

A log is a record of the essential information of your journey. This information must include distances and bearings, and may include any other information which the log writer considers helpful to himself or others.

Distances for log making in cross-country travel are calculated from the factors of rate of travel, and time.

Rate of travel varies. On open undulating country with short grass underfoot a walker will average a mile in between seventeen and twenty minutes, but in steep rocky country overgrown with scrub and thick growth underfoot a mile in sixty minutes might be good speed, and I have known places in New Guinea where one had to cut one's path through thick pit-pit (a giant grass up to 12 feet high) and there a mile forward would not be made in eight hours.

The following table may be considered a fair guide to walking paces. Remember there is a tendency to overestimate rate of travel.

COUNTRY	Time to walk one mile	
	Minimum	Maximum
Open country, firm underfoot, level or slightly undulating	15 minutes	20 minutes
Scrubby country, rocky underfoot, 50 to 100 ft. ascents and descents	24 ,,	30 ,,
Scrub and jungle. Steep ascents and descents (1-10 to 1-3 grade), rocky or bad underfoot	30 ,,	40 ..
Long steep ascents and descents of 800 to 1000 ft. or more, rocky or uneven underfoot	60 ,,	90 ,,

These figures are for an active man laden with a 30 to 40 lb. pack. With heavier loads the maximum time would apply. Rate of progress can be checked by each individual walker for himself. He can assume that 110 paces equal 100 yards, on level walking, and by multiplying the time to walk 100 yards by 17½ he will have a very accurate indication of his walking speed per mile.

In climbing or descending rocky or broken ground his

pace will be very much shorter and slower, and the walker will take about 150 to 170 paces (depending upon slope) to equal 100 yards. On very steep slopes there may be 200 paces or more per 100 yards of lateral distance. '

Time of course can be obtained from your watch, or, failing that, from your sun clock - sun compass (previously drawn on your map) or drawn on the piece of paper on which you are keeping your log. A log is kept most easily by recording the information in vertical colums.

Time	Rate of Travel	Distance Miles	True Bearing	Observation
8.30	$3\frac{1}{2}$	3	84	Open grassland very good walking. High ranges to east about 4 miles. River 1 mile south.
9.30	2	1	197	Climbed steep saddle to range crest. Very rough and stony. Grade on top 1-8. River $\frac{1}{2}$ mile south at foot of range.
10.00	$2\frac{1}{2}$	$3\frac{3}{4}$	110	Range crest stony under-foot. Many small crests to be climbed. Sides too steep to detour. River going south-east along foot of range. Range rising to east.

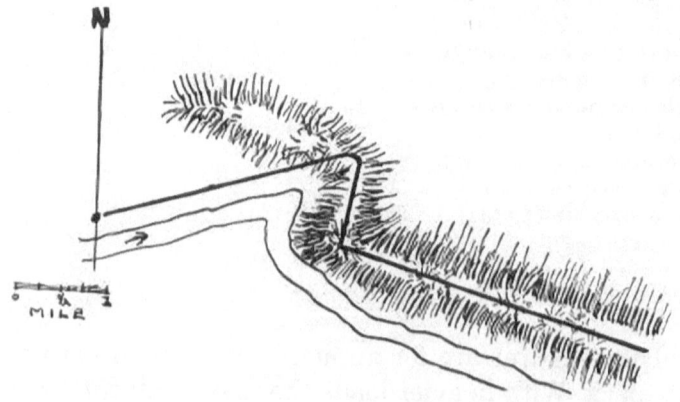

This information is later plotted, and in this form it becomes a chart of your route. With this chart plotted you are never lost, because you always know where you are in relation to the point from which you started. It was in this manner that early explorers recorded their routes into unknown lands.

Choice of Route

Given a free choice it is always advisable in cross-country travel to choose a route up spurs and ranges and down streams, unless in very mountainous country. By following this principle there is less likelihood of getting lost for the simple reason that all spurs lead to the main range crest, and all streams lead to the main river course. By travelling down spurs, or up rivers it is very easy to take the wrong spur; or follow the wrong watercourse and so in a few miles to find oneself hopelessly bushed.

This applies to country which is sparsely populated. Therefore before setting out across country it is advisable to carefully study your map, and plan your route, remembering all the time the general rule to choose if possible, a route up spurs and down rivers.

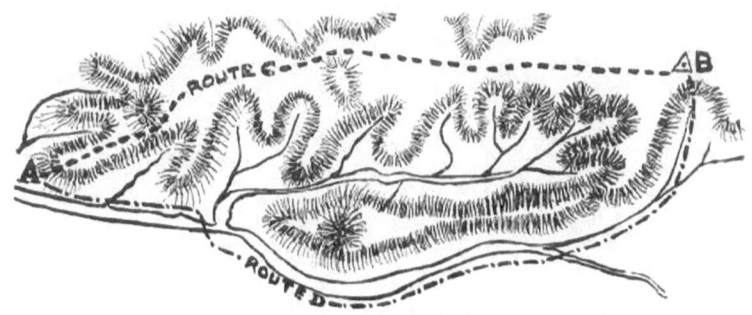

This sketch map will show you how very easy it is to get "bushed" by either travelling down a series of spurs, or up a watershed. The wise bushman, wishing to go from A to B, will go by the route C rather than by the route D.

You will find these alternatives are often presented to you in cross-country travel.

Map Reading

While many maps show man-made features such as prominent buildings, roads, railways, and canals. It is advisable to read the ground shape of the land and not place too much reliance on man-made works. The surface of the land will never change, but man-made constructions may vanish.

The most obvious natural features are ranges and rivers. The ranges may be very steep, or gently sloping, and to show this map makers either use 'contour' lines or hatchuring.

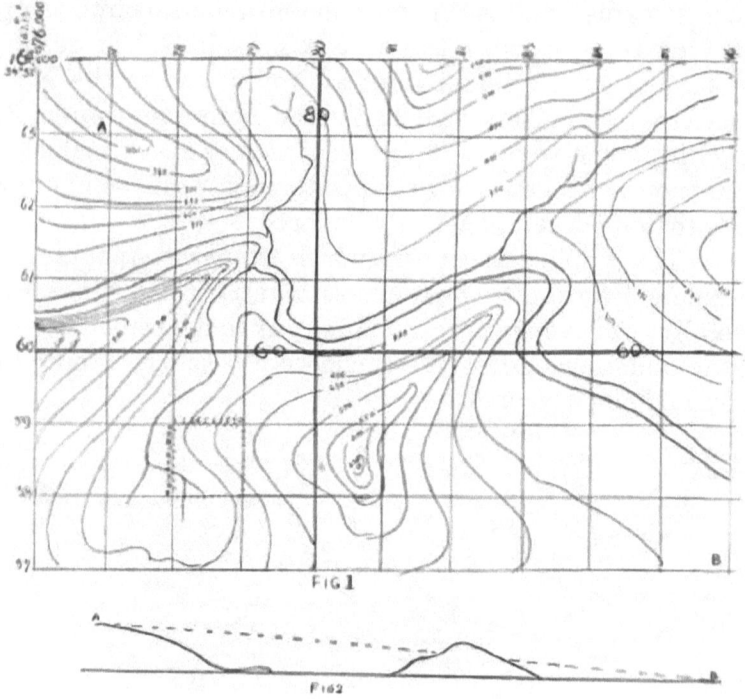

FIG 1

FIG 2

Contour lines are imaginary lines parallel in height and with an equal height separating one height line from the next. By correctly reading contours on a map you can tell if one hill is convex or concave in its slope. If concave, you can see the bottom of the hill from the top, unless of course intervening vegetation limits your visibility. With convex slopes you cannot see the lower grades because the curvature of the slope cuts off your field of vision.

The end of the spur in top left position of the map shown is a convex slope, and the slope east from the hill bottom centre is a concave slope.

A convex slope shows the contour lines closer together at the foot of the hill, and wider apart at the top, while a concave slope shows the contour lines farther apart toward the lower slopes.

Position on a map is always given by a 'map reference.'

These are a series of numbers which indicate the square referred to. You will see in the top left corner of the map (Fig. 1) numbers reading vertically and also other numbers reading horizontally. These numbers are always shown on military maps, which you are more likely to use than others.

The vertical figures indicate the longitude (shown as 147 degrees 15 minutes), and the other figures 976,000 are the number of yards from the 'base line' of that section of country. Reading to the right from the top left corner each smaller square is indicated by the last two THOUSAND numbers, 77, 78, etc. Each square is 1000 yards (unless marked otherwise—see the map scale for this information). The same rule applies to the horizontal numbering; on this column is shown the latitude of the line (in this case 34 degrees 50 minutes south of the equator). Map references are read from west to east first and from south to north, so that the figures 78.58 mean that you look along the grid line 78 until you find the square starting 58, and the reference is within that 1000 yard square. Each thousand yard square is divided again into ten smaller squares, each of which is 100 yards. This gives a six-figure reference 782.583. and you will find that this is the fork of the creek in the third square second row from the bottom.

Now see if 806.584 is the top of a hill?

Map reading when done correctly allows you to build up in your mind a picture of what you could see from any given position. If you were on the spur at A 768.632, could you see the position B at 858.572? In the lower diagram (fig. 2) the elevations between A and B have been plotted. The tongue of hill running north-east through 81.59 and 82.60 would interrupt your view of B from A.

A military map also shows you a 'legend,' which are symbols indicating vegetation, water, and roads, etc. This is generally given at the foot of the map, and assists you in building up in your mind a complete picture of the country.

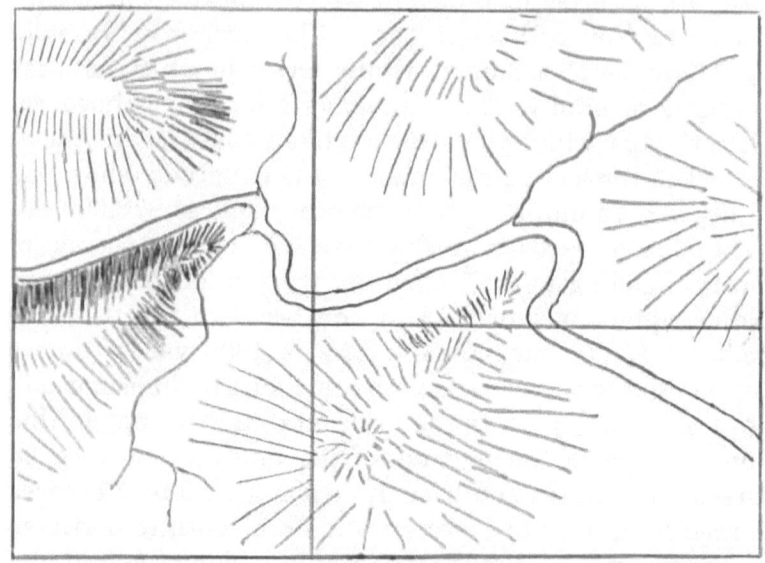

Hatchuring, instead of contour lines, is used by some map makers to give an indication of the nature of the country. Fig. 3 would be a hatchured map of the same country shown in fig. 1. In hatchuring thick strokes close together indicate very steep grades, while thin strokes far apart indicate gentle slopes. In many European maps the hatchurings are definite, thick strokes very close together might mean a slope of 1 in 2, to 1 in 3; thick strokes farther apart a slope of 1 in 4 to 1 in 6; thin strokes close together 1 in 8 to 1 in 10. These of course may be also expressed in degree of slope (1 in 56 grade equals a one degree slope).

The Sun Compass - Sun Clock

Direction and time can both be obtained by drawing a sun compass - sun clock on your map. Trace off overleaf for the latitude line nearest to your map, and it will be both a compass and a clock for you. With a sun compass - sun clock, when you have any one of the following you can discover the other two.

1. A watch to get correct time.

2. A reliable compass.

3. A map correctly oriented (that is laid in the ground so that the features drawn on the map correspond exactly with the recognisable ground features).

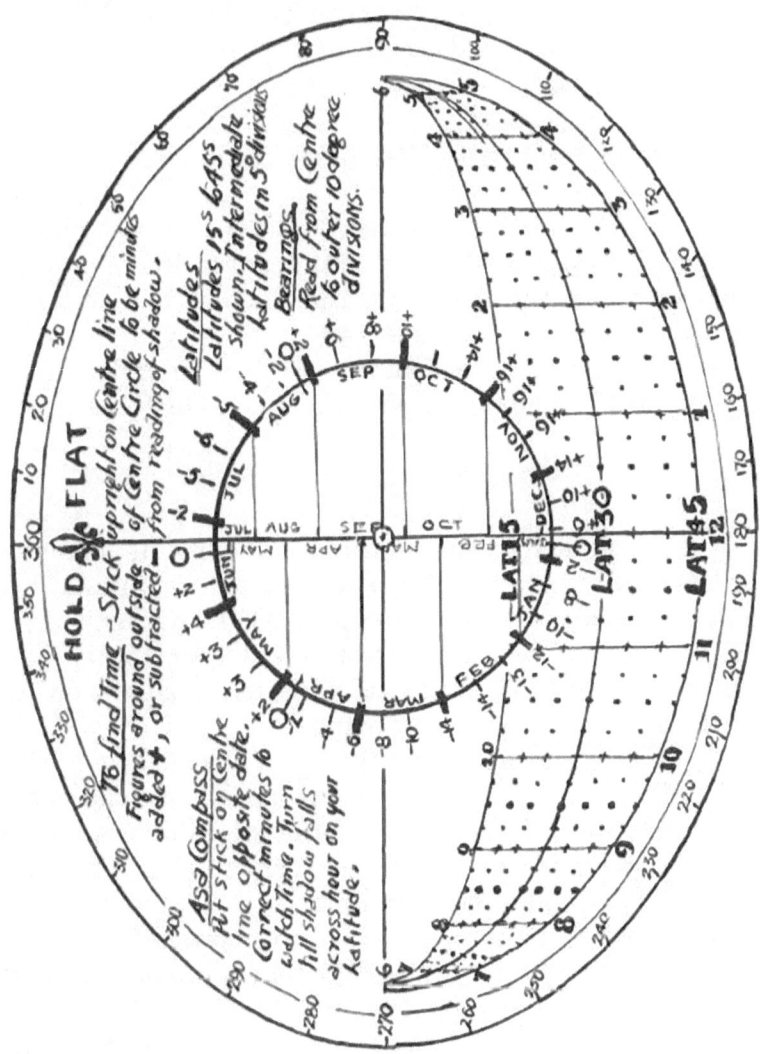

When You Are Able to Orient Your Map Correctly

The north-south line of your sun compass will correspond with the north-south of your map, and your time is read and corrected as explained in the preceding instructions.

To orient your map select two, or better, three, recognisable land features, and identify these on your map. Turn your map until the identified features exactly correspond in direction with the ground features. When this is done your map should exactly fit all the ground plan visible from your position.

When You Have a Watch Set To Correct Time

Place a thin shadow stick on the centre line of the sun compass which must be held flat, opposite the appropriate date, and turn the map until the shadow falls across the adjusted time on the latitude line.

When you have done this your map will be set to TRUE north, and oriented with the ground features.

When You Have a Compass

Place your compass on the map with its axis along TRUE north line, and turn both map and compass till the compass needle is pointing to the MAGNETIC north of your map. (This may be east or west of TRUE north depending where you are.) The magnetic variation is shown on ALL Ordinance Survey (Military) maps.

When you have done this, hold the shadow stick on the north-south line of the sun clock opposite the appropriate date and where the shadow of the stick falls across the latitude line is local sun time. To correct to STANDARD or CLOCK time make the correction for the equation of time shown opposite the date, and also the correction for longitude by deducting four minutes for each degree you are east of the longitude of standard time, or adding four minutes for each degree you are west. (When east of the longitude or standard time the sun is earlier, and when west the sun is later.)

When the magnetic of your compass exactly points to the magnetic north of your map, then your map is correctly oriented.

Weather Lore

An infallible weather forecast, if a change of weather is coming up, is in the nautical couplet:

"When the rain is before the wind, your topsail halyards better mind,

But when the wind is before the rain, then hoist your topsails up again."

In plain words this says that when rain comes first without wind then expect a long period of bad weather with high winds and heavy rain. But when wind comes first and is followed immediately by rain, then fine weather will follow at short notice.

Many people are trapped by bad weather in the bush every year, and if they but knew of this simple weather sign they could be prepared, and get out to a position of safety before really bad weather sets in.

Another infallible weather signal is the appearance of cumulus nimbus cloud, a foreteller of thunderstorms. While a greenish light in the sky preceding a thunderstorm is an almost certain sign of heavy hail.

Clouds and Their reading

CIRRUS

CIRRO-CUMULUS

CUMULUS

CUMULUS-NIMBUS

Cirrus, this is the "mare's tail" sky of the landsman, shows as long threads or wisps of cloud. This is the highest of all cloud formations, and is a sign of a "high" barometrical pressure, which means fine weather.

Cirro Stratus, and Cirro Cumulus. In these clouds the former is long wispy cloud, and in the latter rounded small cloud the typical "mackerel" sky. Both are indicators of a high barometric pressure, and fine weather.

Cumulus and Cumulus Nimbus. Cumulus is the high white piled-up masses of cloud seen in summer. When streaked with horizontal bands it is Cumulus Nimbus, or thunder cloud, a sign of coming storms, which may be of short duration, or may indicate a change in the weather generally.

Nimbus. This is the grey ragged cloud which uniformly covers the sky. It is the true rain cloud, and an indication of low barometric pressure and rainy weather.

Storm Scud. This is formless masses of very low cloud driven fast before the wind. It is a sign of very low barometric pressure, and continuing bad weather.

Carrying gear

The first thing in travel is the method of carrying your gear. The conventional pack or rucksack need not be described in this column, which concerns itself with improvisation, and therefore only those methods which call for no "shop-made" gear will be given.

The Swag

The swag, proverbial Australian means of carrying a heavy load, is one of the best methods in existence. It is simply made and very easily carried. It has the advantage of being extremely well balanced, two-thirds of the weight being carried behind the body, and about one-third in front. The result is that the carrier walks completely upright. Clothes, tent, bedding and the gear not wanted for the day's walk are carried in the swag at the back, while the food and cooking utensils and day's needs are in the "dilly" bag in front. Because of this the swag is not opened during the day but the dilly bag, attached to the front and right at your hand, is immediately accessible.

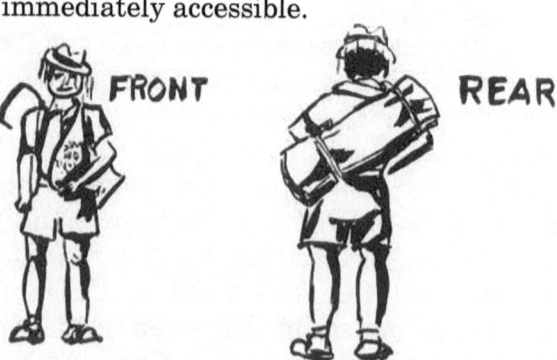

FRONT   REAR

The only components for a swag are a swag strap, two binding straps and a dilly bag. The swag strap, preferably of soft leather, should be about two feet six inches long and a couple of inches wide; the two binding straps can be of any strong material such as rope, or a plaited cord, or a narrow leather strap. The dilly bag can be a sugar or flour bag, some two feet long, and twelve to fifteen inches wide.

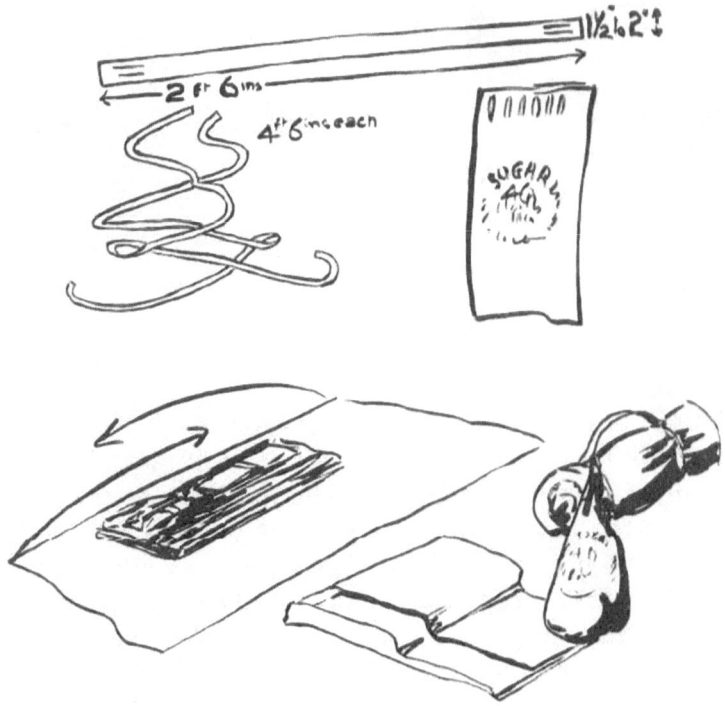

Laying out the gear for a swag, and rolling it and tying on the dilly bag.

These are the components for a swag. The swag strap should be soft and, if need arises, can be easily woven or plaited from strong grass, vines, bark strips or other material as indicated in the Handbook titled "Bush Ropemaking". A soft leather strap is ideal.

Half the knack of carrying a swag consists in knowing how to "swing" it. Lay the roll, with the dilly bag extended in front of you, and then put the arm farthest away from the dilly bag through the swag strap. Heave the roll towards your back, and swing the body towards the swag, so that the dilly bag flies up and out. Duck the opposite shoulder, and catch the swinging dilly bag on it. The swag strap will then lie over one shoulder and the dilly bag over the other, with the swag roll carried at an angle across the back.

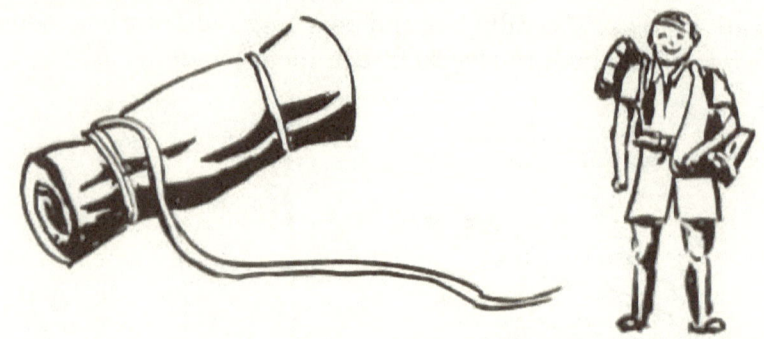

The alternative swag. Note the long strap and the position when the swag is "swung."

An alternative method of carrying the swag is to use two straps, one about 3 ft. 6 ins. long and the other about six ft. long. Both straps should be about an inch and a quarter wide and of strong soft material. The roll is made as for the swag, and the long strap is tied securely about five inches from one end of the roll. Five inches from the other end of the roll the other strap is fastened with the dilly bag held in position by the strap.

The swag is lifted to the left shoulder with the dilly bag in front and the roll at the back, the neck of the dilly bag hanging over the left shoulder. The long strap is passed on top of the right shoulder, and then under the armpit and around the back, and tied to a loop at the bottom corner of the dilly bag. This type of swag prevents the dilly bag from swaying' and is preferred by some "bushmen,"

To roll the swag, lay your groundsheet or swag cover flat on the ground, and then fold your blankets to a width of about thirty inches by about fifteen to twenty. Spare clothes are laid lengthways on top, with your other gear. The sides of the groundsheet are folded in, and the whole is rolled from the blanket end to the free side, into a tight roll. If a tent is being taken this in turn is rolled in the tent. The two binding straps are laid six to eight inches from either end, that is 18 inches to 24 inches apart.

The two binding cords pass through the loops of the swag strap and are tied tightly about six to eight inches from either end of the roll. The food, cooking utensils, and daily needs are put in the dilly bag, and the neck of this is tied right at the junction of the binding strap with the swag strap, or alternatively a series of cuts in the neck of the bag can be made and the binding cord passed through these so that the bag is tight to the roll. If this is done it is a good idea to make a cut down the side of the bag for about twelve inches so that the contents can be taken out without removing the bag itself from the binding straps.

The Adirondack Pack

This is an easily improvised method of carrying heavy loads and an Adirondack pack can be made in less than half an hour. Select two light widely splayed hooks, with the arm of the hook 1 ft. 6 inches to 2 ft. long, and the shank portion three or tour feet in length. It is better to use dead wood, which is well seasoned. This is lighter. A number of short straight sticks are lashed to the inside edge of the shanks above the arms, and two straps are woven or plaited, and tied to the lower end of the shank and again about eighteen inches from the lower end. The two shanks should be about fifteen inches apart where the straps are at the upper end.

Showing an Adirondack pack, and how the load is carried

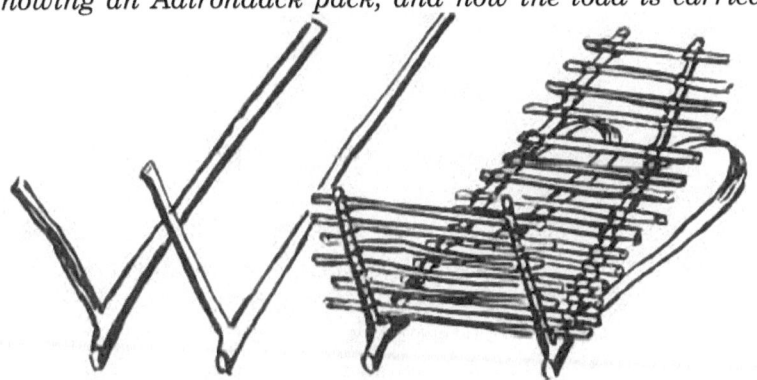

high on the shoulders. If desired a head band can be used to steady the load.

Pannier Pack

A pannier, eighteen inches square at the mouth, and two feet to two feet six inches deep, is woven from canes, rushes or any convenient pliable material. To this two straps woven from some pliable material are secured at the top, and eighteen inches below. The gear to be carried is loaded into the pannier.

River Crossings

One of the principal hazards in cross-country travel are river crossings.

For the crossing of rivers, and if the walker is a swimmer, the pack can be wrapped in a groundsheet which has its corners and loose-folds tied together. This will support the traveller who holds the pack in his hands and by kicking with his legs he can cross safely with his pack. It is advisable to tie a short length of cord to the wrist so that if the pack slips from the hands it can be recovered.

It is inadvisable to try to swim a river while wearing walking boots. These should be taken off and placed with the pack in the groundsheet. If a party of four or more are crossing, tie two or three packs together after each has been put in its groundsheet. One party stands by on the bank while the other party crosses.

Always place a layer of fern or grass or small brush beneath your pack before folding the groundsheet on it. If your groundsheet leaks slightly, this precaution will give your pack an inch or two clearance and keep it dry. With a frame rucksack, lay your frame uppermost—with a swag, place your swag roll and dilly bag side by side before folding the groundsheet.

A method of improvised water travel for poor swimmers or non-swimmers is by the use of two calico ration bags inflated, and used as water wings. These will easily support a human body in the water, and the non-swimmer can be taken across the river with absolute safety.

A pair of long drill pants can also be used to support a nonswimmer. The trousers are wetted, and the cuffs tied in a thumb knot, and then, holding the fly to the front with the legs hanging behind the back, the trousers are swung up, forward and then suddenly down into the water, so that air is trapped in the legs. The crutch is put across the chest, and the two legs under the arms. By this means any nonswimmer can be taken across a river with safety. The experienced swimmer who may have to travel for some distance along a river will find his trousers or long-sleeved shirt a veritable life-saver if used in this manner. He can tread water while inflating the legs, and they will remain buoyant for from ten minutes to a couple of hours, depending on the material from which they are made. One aircrew man who bailed out into the sea kept himself afloat for more than thirty-eight hours by this means.

Rafts

Small bolsters made of ground sheets can be rolled up and lashed together if there is a party travelling together. These make an excellent raft, stable and buoyant, for either ferrying the party over the river or for actual travel along the river itself.

Showing how to make a bolster, and how the bolsters are lashed together into a raft.

Rafting is a practical means of water travel. The raft is built up from dry driftwood, and can be secured and made tight by lashing. In still water the raft can be poled along if the water is shallow. In travelling upstream it must be towed if the current is strong, or if travelling downstream, a "kellick" made either from a log of hardwood or a heavy stone is dragged astern in rapids. A sweep or long paddle ahead enables the raft to be steered because the water sweeping past the structure travels faster than the raft and this provides "steerageway" in reverse.

A raft, witii kellick and sweep.

Coracle

When a canvas or heavy duck fly, or waterproof tent, or Japara or Willesden cloth tent is available, an excellent Coracle or boat can be made easily and quickly. The dimensions of the coracle are determined by the size of cover when laid flat. This is first measured and an allowance of at least eighteen inches for "turn up" is deducted from each of the two sides and the ends.

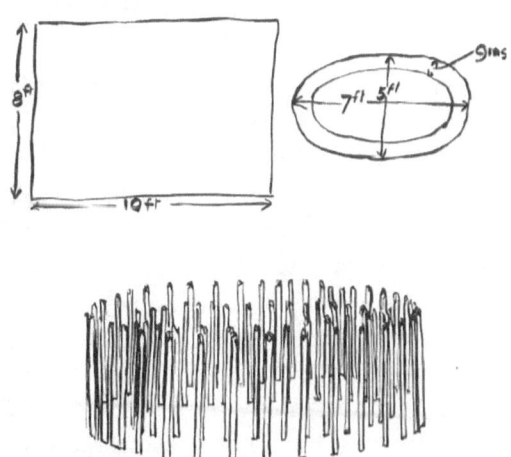

Sticks in double row around the two ovals. This is the appearance of the frame structure for coracle building.

To these dimensions an oval is drawn on the ground, and nine inches inside this oval a second line is drawn. A number of straight sticks each about two feet long are cut and these are driven into the ground every six or eight inches around the two ovals.

Between these double rows of stakes green or half-dead fern, light branches and other waste bush material is packed to a height of about fifteen inches. This material does not need to be packed very tightly, but should be firm. When the required height is reached the wall is bound with vines, strips of bark, or other available material. A few long sticks, just a few inches shorter than the length of the wall, are placed lengthways, with a number of shorter cross sticks on top. These are tied to the top lines around the wall.

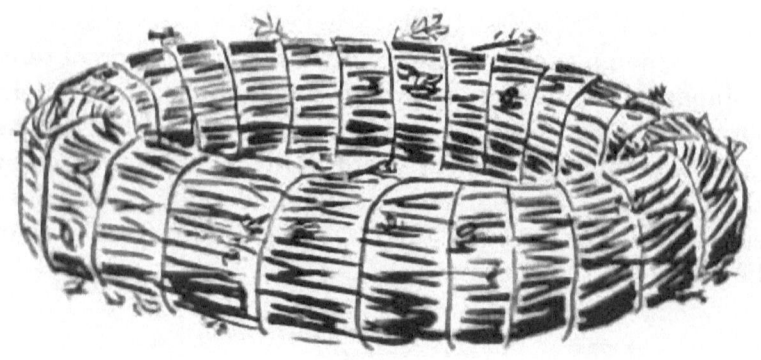

This is the wall of the coracle complete, but without the floor sticks.

The canvas which is to be the cover for the coracle is laid flat alongside the structure. It is necessary to put a six-inch (unpacked) layer of fern, grass or other soft material over the whole of the centre area'. The coracle wall is lifted straight up from the double wall of sticks, turned over, and laid on the centre of the canvas. It may be found desirable to lay it diagonally rather than square. The sides are turned up, and tied over the wall to the floor sticks, and when this is done the coracle is ready for launching.

This is a completed coracle launched. A coracle six feet by four wide with fifteen-inch walls will easily support four men.

Care must be taken to sit inside the walls and not on them. Any weight pressing on the walls will tend to break them down, and allow water to flow over the sides. A coracle is perfectly stable, and when poling or paddling along a shallow river it will be found more convenient to stand. For long trips paddles, as for a canoe, can be used, or even oars lashed to the top of the wall in place of rowlocks will enable good progress to be made.

Long river journeys can be made by coracle—travelling in it by day, and at night removing the coracle cover from the walls and pitching it as a tent.

Bark Canoe

Where timber is plentiful, and the destruction of a green tree is permissible, a bark canoe can be made. The essential quality is that the bark must not be brittle, that it shall be reasonably pliable (considering its thickness), and that it be fibrous, and easily stripped from the tree. Also the barrel of the tree must be straight and free from branches and knot holes. The bark is cut around the lower portion of the tree, and then a ladder is made and it is ringed again fifteen or more feet above the lowest ring. The two rings are joined with a series of zig-zag cuts running straight along the barrel from one ring to the other.

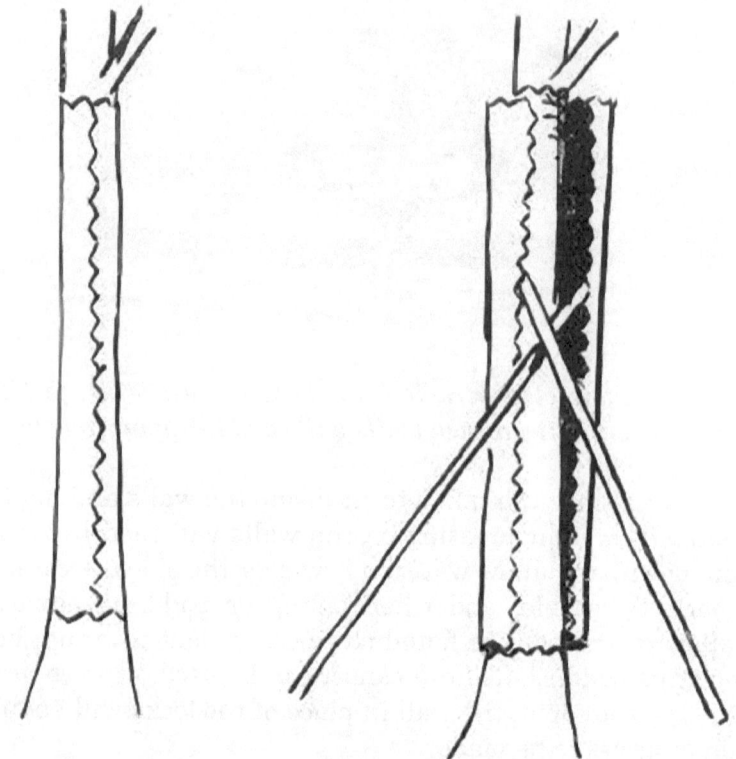

A tree ringed and ready for the bark to be removed.

The entire sheet of bark is carefully removed in one piece by means of two long poles chisel shaped at one end which is inserted (one on either side) in the vertical cut. By working these poles up and down under the bark, it will gradually be lifted and spread, coming off the tree in one sheet. This is spread with the opening on the lower side, and a quick fire of leaves is lit inside. The heat from this fire will drive the sap, in the form of steam, through the dry outer bark, and make the sheet more pliable. When it is flexible, the whole sheet if possible should be turned inside out after the fire treatment. Do not attempt this if there is any sign that the sheet of bark will split; instead allow the rough outside to be outside of your canoe.

The two ends are drawn together as closely as possible, and six inches to fifteen inches from the ends a series of holes are cut with a sharp knife. These holes should be cut in a zig-zag pattern. Vine, or very tough bark strips or other strong tying material is laced through these holes and the lacing pulled tight to draw the ends together. Inside, the ends are packed with clay which will make them completely watertight.

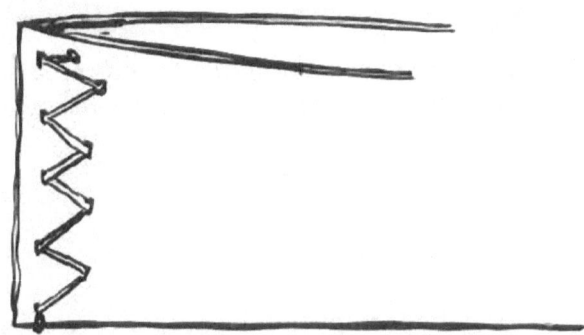

The first stage in the construction of a bark canoe. The ends have been drawn together, and the inside is packed with clay.

Spreaders are required across the centre of the canoe, and to fit these, two split pieces of round timber about two feet long and at least four inches across are cut. Holes are cut in the bark near the centre of the canoe at the top and through these the lashing material for the spreader ends are lashed. These two spreader ends are nicked in the centre to provide a seating for the spreader itself. The spreader is simply a straight strong stick wide enough to keep the centre of the bark canoe spread open; the ends are seated against the two nicks cut in the spreader ends.

Except for paddles the canoe is now ready for launching. Paddles are shaped out of any convenient straight-grained dead timber with the blade about six inches wide if possible.

A bark canoe must be kept in the water all the time. If taken out or allowed to dry it will almost certainly split or crack and be unserviceable. If left in the water it should remain in serviceable condition for two or three years.

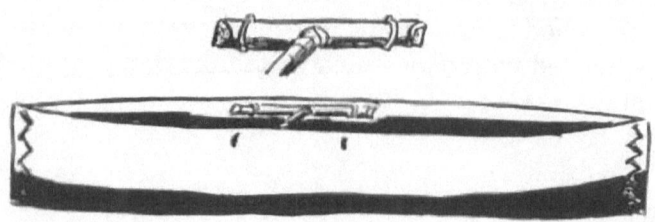

The finished canoe. Note how the spreader ends are secured in position, and how the spreader sits in the nicked cuts.

Health

Care of Feet

It is vitally important to take proper care of your feet on a walking trip. A small blister can rub away and become a raw spot, and you will be immobilised and your progress both painful and slow.

If the feet show signs of being tender, the skin can be toughened up by urinating on the feet. When blisters threaten or develop, sticking plaster will prevent their further development, and offer immediate relief. The best treatment for a blister when it has already formed is to thread a piece of clean cotton through the blistered skin, cutting off the thread a quarter inch on either side of its point of entry. This will drain the fluid from the blister but prevent the air from entering. Cover the blister with sticking plaster or a bandage.

Ingrowing toenails are another cause of foot trouble. Immediate relief can be obtained by scraping the top of the toenail either with a file, rasp, the sharp edge of a knife, or even a piece of broken glass. The top of the nail should be scraped until it is sufficiently thin to be easily depressed with the tip of your finger.

Corns, of course, can be pared down, but a reputable make of corn plaster, and avoiding tight-fitting shoes, is the best way to keep free from these troubles.

Twisted ankles are a common ailment in rocky country.

If the twist is not too severe the best thing is to keep

on the move, gradually getting the ankle into working order through exercise. If the twist is severe, sufficient to make the walker completely immobile, alternate bathings with very hot water and cold water will stimulate the blood flow, and give the patient some relief. After this treatment apply a tight bandage and the patient should be able to limp along.

When walking along river courses it is not advisable to remove your boots. Most riverbeds are stony, and frequently the stones are slippery with algae and other slimy growths, so that when walking barefooted one is likely to take a sudden fall. Also the water-rounded stones on the sole of the foot can become extremely tiring after a short distance.

Water will not damage your boots, but drying them out by a fire later will, so never, never put your boots by a fire to dry. Far better to leave them wet. They will be wet again after five minutes walking through damp bush in any case. When you try to dry boots out before a fire you also dry out the natural oils in the leather, and your boots become stiff and hard. If they are put too close to the fire they will burn.

If your boots become too severely damaged to use, you can walk barefooted on grass and sandy earth, but if you try barefooted walking on stony roads your feet will soon go to pieces and you may be badly crippled. Improvised mocassins can be made from the soft inner bark of several species of trees.

Bush Remedy for Stomach and Bowel Upsets

A very simple remedy for many abdominal troubles is to chew and swallow a piece of charcoal every two or three hours. A lump about the size of a threepenny piece should give some relief if the trouble is similar to a gastric or bilious upset. A frequent cause of stomach ache is the drinking of very cold water while hot through walking. It is a good precaution under such conditions to drink very slowly, and warm each mouthful of water in the mouth before swallowing it.

Cleanliness and Food

Cleanliness of eating utensils is very important. These should be washed immediately after a meal, and left exposed if possible to the sunlight after washing. If there is any doubt about your meat being safe to eat, then assume it is bad, rather than take the chance. The safest way to carry meat is to partly cook it while you know it is still fresh and safe. Cooking will destroy the harmful bacteria of decay, for a period. Such items of mixed meat as sausages are best cooked before you leave home, and then carried in the fat in which they were cooked. This will preserve them for four days to a week, depending upon the weather.

Butter can be carried in the hottest weather if packed in a container which in turn is put in the middle of your flour. The flour will act as an insulator, and keep the butter at whatever temperature you packed it.

Care of the Eyes

Nature has provided your eyes with a most effective germ killer, your tears. A tear will kill most bacteria and is a defence for your eyes.

Despite this natural protection, your eyes may suffer from glare or from entry of a particle of dust or sand. To protect your eyes from glare, tie a bootlace, or a thin strip of bark or some dark-coloured material, across your face just below your eyes. This will break the glare from the ground and give you almost immediate eye relief.

If a particle of dust or sand enters the eye do not rub the particular eye affected. Rub the opposite eye. Rubbing will stimulate the flow of tears and these will help to wash out the irritating matter. If this is not effective, try cupping water in your hands and immerse your sore eye in the cupped water. This will generally prove effective.